The Sordid Lives of Jesus' Ancestors

by Alice Newsome

Every family has skeletons in their closets

Jesus' family does too!

The Sordid Lives of Jesus' Ancestors:

Every family has skeletons in their closets Jesus' family does too!

By Alice Newsome

Unless otherwise indicated, all Scripture quotations are taken from the King James Version (KJV) of the Bible.

Scripture quotations are taken from the Holy Bible, New Living Translation, copyright ©1996, 2004, 2007, 2013, 2015 by Tyndale House Foundation. Used by permission of Tyndale House Publishers, Inc., Carol Stream, Illinois 60188. All rights reserved.

Book layout assisted by Diverse Skills Center – www.diverseskillscenter.com

Lutz, FL

ISBN 13: 978-0-692-87136-2

Foreword

There is a chorus of a song in a church hymnal that says ------
"I am so glad that Jesus loves me, Jesus loves me! Jesus loves
me!

I am so glad that Jesus loves me, Jesus loves even me."

The Bible says: "There is no difference, for all have sinned
and come short of the Glory of God." Some may feel their
"coming short" is viewed more dishonorable than somebody
else' "come short." One thing is very clear ------we have all
dishonored the Lord in one fashion or another.

A voice demanding to be heard, Alice Newsome's first novel
will grip you from beginning to end as she tells us about
some of the women in Jesus' family tree who had one degree
or multiple degrees of shortcomings, but God turned the
shortcoming into a great outcome. She tells a well written,
well-researched story. It is written with humor, grace and
great respect for the power of womanhood. Alice's voice is
strong, confident and distinctive as she makes each character
come alive. You, the reader, will suddenly be plunged into
the hearts and souls of each character. Even though the
customs, traditions and general way of life are taken from an
Old Testament period, Alice has a fresh way of bringing
them to life so that they are witty, wise and uplifting in our
21st Century.

There is an old proverb that says, "There is nothing new
under the sun." As you are transported back into history

with each story, you will find this to be a consistent statement. The situations and circumstances may be different today, but as women, our emotions, our desires, and our feelings remain the same.

You may be able to identify with the heart of some of these women. At the least, maybe, you can feel what they felt to try to understand why they did what they did. Wrapped around it all is the hand and leading of God as He works out His Sovereign Plan in each of their lives. Understand how He's not stopped working in the lives of women today. If He did it for them, He will do it for us.

To read Alice's book on the lives of Tamar, Rahab, Ruth, Bathsheba and other women, should make us readers hunger for the revelation of God's Plan in our own lives.

Jeremiah 29:11(NIV) says: "For I know the plans I have for you," says the Lord. "They are plans for good and not disaster, to give you a future and a hope". In those days when you pray, I will listen. If you look to me in earnest, you will find me when you seek me, I will be found by you."

Enjoy!

Elder Brenda McWhorter

Special Thanks

I am grateful to God for the gifts, talents, and abilities He has placed within me, so I say thank you, Lord! I am overwhelmed at this moment in my life.

These words are an inadequate expression of my love and appreciation for all that you mean to me. You are an extension of me, we are joined at the heart. Thank you so much family: Mykal, Momma, Marlena, Brandi, and Shyra. I love you much!

Thank you to my grandchildren SaMyah, Michael, Chyna, Casen, Caleb, and Xavier. You are my heart!

Thank you to my sisters: Annette, Angie, and Theresa. I am grateful for each of you and the contributions you have added to my life.

Thank you, Telisa Marshall, for sharing your comments and expertise. Your input has proven to be an invaluable asset in the completion of this book.

Thank you to Mary Martin, Kianna Storm, Guilene Philmore, Toni Ferrille, Shyra Newsome, Marlene Leary, and Brandi Brown for lending their images for the illustrations in this book.

A very special thanks to the illustrator for this book, Mykal Newsome

Table of Contents

Introduction

If it was possible to design your perfect adult offspring before conception, what characteristics would he or she possess?

Sex_____   Height _____

Weight _____

Bones _____

Head shape _____

Body shape _____

Shoe size _____

Hand size _____

Skin color _____

Skin texture _____

Hair color _____

Hair texture _____

Hair length _____

Eye color _____

Eye shape _____

Describe eyelashes _____

Describe nose _____

Describe lips _____

Describe teeth _____

Personality traits _____

Special skills set _____

Nationality _____

Language _____

Intelligence level _____

Other _____

_____

_____

_____

_____

_____

_____

_____

As you contemplate designing your perfect adult offspring, consider the characteristics God chose in His masterpiece. Did you place more value on their physical appearance or inner character traits? How does your design compare to God's?

Since God is the Creator of heaven and earth, He is keenly aware of the composition and characteristics of every person ever born on this planet. God had access to traits from the very best gene pools in the universe to create His Perfect Son, Jesus.

Jesus was designed to be the Son of God as well as the Son of Man. To be the Son of Man, Jesus had to be born of a woman. What characteristics would this woman possess?

It's only natural to expect the mother of God's Son to be exceptionally beautiful, charming, graceful and elegant. By my standards, she should be the epitome of human perfection, she must be as close to perfect as possible. Yes, she would be a royal virgin princess.

The man recognized as Jesus' earthly father should possess moral excellence as well. He should be a man of high standings in the community with royal status, perhaps a prince, or at least, a very successful businessman.

In my imagination, the Son of God would be perfect in every way. He would be the most handsome man to have ever lived on the earth. He would be tall and gorgeous with flawless skin, beautiful hair, and wonderful eyes. He would possess a kind and sensitive spirit, yet he would be strong, decisive, and very courageous with a beautiful smile.

So, what did Jesus look like? Was he 6'3" with a chiseled physique? Did he have long flowing blonde hair encircled with a halo? Did he have a manicured beard with piercing baby blue eyes?

These characteristics do not describe Jesus' physical appearance at all. In fact, he was not much to look at.

> *He hath no form nor comeliness; and when we shall see him, there is no beauty that we should desire him. (Isaiah 53:2b)*

God designed his son to be physically unattractive or common-looking. There was nothing about his appearance to cause one to lust after him or have a crush on him. He was not the type that people naturally gravitated to because of his good looks.

Although Jesus was not a "stud" I still would expect the Son of God to be of royal descent. His pure bloodline should be traceable back to Adam.

There are two accounts in Scripture detailing the names of Jesus' ancestors. Luke chapter three traces Jesus' bloodline back to Adam while Matthew chapter one traces it back to Abraham.

The Bible is filled with interesting historical facts. It marks the beginning and end of time, as well as the lives of people in between. God uses the Bible to tell us about Himself and His interactions with men and women who lived long ago.

I must admit that sometimes it is boring to read the Bible, especially the begets and the hard to pronounce names. However, when you associate the Biblical names with their stories, the Bible can read like your favorite novel.

Matthew chapter one is filled with "begets" and hard to pronounce names. It is a historical recording of Jesus' ancestors beginning with Abraham. Most of the names listed in this text are male, however, dispersed among the men's names are the names of 4 women. This book takes a detailed look at the ancestors of Jesus and focuses on the women in his family tree.

Filled with intrigue and suspense, these Biblical stories capture our attention as we gain insight into the Word of God. As we read, the Bible comes alive with word pictures of another place and time.

My goal is to provide interesting insights into the lives of Jesus' ancestors so that you can easily associate their names with their stories. My hope is to inspire you to read more of the Bible and cultivate a closer relationship with God.

Chapter 1

You Make Me Laugh

> *The book of the generation of Jesus Christ, the son of*
> *David, the son of Abraham. Abraham begat Isaac;*
> *and Isaac begat Jacob; and Jacob begat Judas and*
> *his brethren; (Matthew 1:1-2)*

The story of Jesus' family heritage in Matthew chapter one, starts with the patriarch Abraham. We are first introduced to him as Abram, but God later changes his name to Abraham. Here are God's first recorded instructions to Abram.

> *Now the LORD had said unto Abram, get thee out*
> *of thy country, and from thy kindred, and from thy*
> *father's house, unto a land that I will shew thee:*
> *(Genesis 12:1)*

God told Abram to leave his father's house, his relatives, and his country. Can you imagine uprooting and relocating? All the things you have accumulated over the years must be sold, given away, left behind, or packed up. Moving is a big deal, especially moving out of the country. In addition to this, Abram was not given a clear destination. God wanted Abram to follow His lead and go to an unfamiliar place that would be revealed as he traveled.

God promised to make Abram an abundantly blessed man. He would bless everything associated with him now and in the future. Abram believed God and followed His instructions. He packed his things and left his father's house. Together with his wife Sarai and his nephew Lot, Abram began his journey to follow God. Throughout scripture, I have noticed when God told Abram to do something, he did it immediately.

God's promises to Abram:

• He would be a great nation.

• He would be famous.

• He would be a blessing to others.

• God would bless those who blessed him.

• God would curse those who cursed him.

• All the families of the earth will be blessed through Abram.

That's quite a promise, all families will be blessed through Abram. How was God to accomplish this? Abram did not question God, he believed Him.

In Genesis fifteen, God promised Abram that his descendants would be as numerous as the stars in the sky. Abram was excited about this promise because he really wanted to be a father. He relayed this message to his wife Sarai, and she was ecstatic. They had been married many years, but this one thing eluded Sarai and it was what she wanted most – Abram's children.

They were energized by this news and immediately started working on conception. They tried and tried and tried, but they were unable to conceive. Month after month, Sarai's hope turned to disappointment as she began another menstrual cycle. She had some dark days of feeling down and just plain inadequate. After trying and failing so many times, Sarai lost hope and concluded that God's blessing did not include her. She knew that God was faithful to His word and He would indeed bless Abram with lots of children; but obviously not through her.

In Genesis sixteen, Sarai arranged a second marriage for her husband. Yes, she did. She willingly gave her husband to another woman. In Sarai's mind, the new wife would be a surrogate mother and have children that she could call her very own.

When Sarai presented this plan to Abram, the scripture does not state that Abram thought about it, prayed about it or resisted the idea. He agreed with the plan and married Hagar, Sarai's Egyptian slave. It worked! Hagar became pregnant, had Abram's son and named him Ishmael. I guess Sarai was content because she got what she wanted – or did she?

Well, let's back up a bit to find out. With the confirmation of pregnancy, Hagar became very proud. In just a few short months she successfully accomplished something the first wife repeatedly tried and failed to do for years. She was impregnated with Abram's heir. Hagar started to snub Sarai and disrespect her. I imagine Hagar strutting around the tent patting her pregnant belly and peering at Sarai through squinted eyes with a look of disgust on her face. Sarai was upset and blamed Abram for this mess, but he threw the ball right back in her court. He told her to deal with the problem she created. So, Sarai did just that.

Sarai must have treated Hagar like an unloved stepchild. Home sweet home was now a war zone, and the first wife was winning every battle. Life was so uncomfortable for Hagar that she ran away. She eventually returned with a different attitude. She submitted to Sarai, showed her the respect she deserved, and their home became peaceful again. Later Hagar birthed Abram's son and named him Ishmael.

In Genesis seventeen, when Abram was ninety-nine years old he had a visit from God who made a covenant with him. Abram's part of the agreement was to serve God faithfully and live a blameless life. In exchange for this, God promised Abram that he would father many nations – he would have countless descendants and some of them would be kings! God promised to bless Abram's seed forever. That day God changed Abram's name to Abraham which means father of many nations. That same day, God changed Sarai's name to Sarah. She too would be the mother of many nations and some of her descendants would be kings!

This was an eventful day jammed packed with blessings for Abraham. That spectacular day was etched in his memory for the rest of his life. He laughed so hard when God said that his elderly, menopausal wife Sarah was going to have his baby! When Sarah heard this news, she laughed too!

As Sarah's flabby, old belly became firm and full of life she was overcome with gratitude to God for giving her the opportunity and strength to carry a child in her aged body. Their home was filled with so much love, so much joy, so much happiness, excitement, and laughter. When the baby boy finally arrived, they named him Isaac which means laughter. This was the miracle child of 100-year-old Abraham and his 90-year-old wife Sarah. Baby boy Isaac was surrounded by so much love.

Little Isaac changed Sarah's life. She no longer felt inadequate because she now embraced her own son who nursed at her elderly, plump, milk-filled breast. Sarah was happy and satisfied.

Isaac was the apple of Sarah's eye. He was the only child she would ever have. He was the perfect gift and the answer to many prayers. Sarah loved her son with all her heart and poured herself into him. She was a very protective mom. In Genesis twenty-one, when her stepson Ishmael teased little Isaac, mother hen Sarah wasn't having it. She had that boy and his mother put out, never to return to her house again.

Sarah had everything she wanted, a successful, committed husband, and her miracle son Isaac who was the rightful heir to their fortune.

Sarah spent thirty-seven wonderful years with her beloved Isaac before she died at the ripe old age of one hundred and twenty-seven years old. (Gen 23:1).

Notes

_____

_____

_____

_____

_____

_____

_____

_____

_____

_____

_____

_____

_____

_____

_____

_____

Notes

_____

_____

_____

_____

_____

_____

_____

_____

_____

_____

_____

_____

_____

_____

_____

Notes

_____

_____

_____

_____

_____

_____

_____

_____

_____

_____

_____

_____

_____

_____

_____

Chapter 2

Answered Prayer

> *Abraham begat Isaac; and Isaac begat Jacob; and*
> *Jacob begat Judas and his brethren; (Matthew 1:2)*

Isaac was the only son of his elderly parents, Abraham and Sarah. In fact, he was their miracle child! He was born to a woman who suffered from infertility all her childbearing years. Then, finally after menopause, Sarah was given the gift of motherhood and boy, did she laugh! She was able to enjoy her husband again, experience pregnancy and deliver a son at 90 years old! What a miracle! Can you imagine the smile on Sarah's face as she held Isaac for the first time? Imagine how proud she was as precious little Isaac matured into a strong, handsome young man. I'll bet he was a momma's boy!

Isaac loved his mom and relied on her companionship. They shared many days of joy and laughter. Even though he was a grown man, spending time with his mom was one of Isaac's top priorities. Sarah was a wonderful mother, she poured her years of knowledge into his life and Isaac learned so much from her. She taught him about life, love, and God.

Death came and changed Isaac's life completely, forever. He lost his mother, his confidant, and his friend.

Isaac's heart was broken, he was sad and lonely because he missed his mother so much. Abraham noticed his son's depressed demeanor and decided to do something to change it. He knew that no one could ever replace Sarah in Isaac's life, but his son needed someone to love.

In typical Abraham fashion, when knowing what to do he did it! He called his senior household servant and conveyed that Isaac needed a wife. He gave the servant specific instructions and sent him on a journey back to his hometown and his relatives, to choose a wife for Isaac.

The servant prepared for his journey to find a bride for Isaac. He loaded ten camels with valuable things like gold bracelets, earrings, beautiful fabrics, and clothing. These valuable gifts were for the special chosen young lady and her family. They would serve as a glimpse into the prospective bride's future if she decided to go back home with the servant and marry Isaac.

It was late afternoon when the servant arrived in Abraham's hometown. He was thirsty, so he stopped near a well. While resting, he decided to talk to God.

> *"And he said O LORD God of my master Abraham, I pray thee, send me good speed this day and shew kindness unto my master Abraham. Behold, I stand here by the well of water; and the daughters of the men of the city come out to draw water:"*
>
> *And let it come to pass, that the damsel to whom I shall say, let down thy pitcher, I pray thee, that I may drink; and she shall say, Drink, and I will give thy camels drink also: let the same be she that thou*

*hast appointed for thy servant Isaac; and thereby
shall I know that thou hast shewed kindness unto
my master. (Genesis 24:12-14)*

Before he finished praying, a young woman came to the well
with a water jar on her shoulder. She gave the servant water
and offered water to his camels. As he sipped the water, he
watched the woman closely to see if she was "the one."
Watering a camel was no easy feat, yet this woman
continuously worked, filling trough after trough with
enough water to quench the thirst of ten camels.

In exchange for her services, the servant gave the young lady
a nose ring and two gold bracelets. As they talked about her
family, he learned that her name was Rebekah and she
happened to be Abraham's great niece! The servant was
overwhelmed and amazed by the power of God to quickly
answer his prayer. Right in front of him stood the answer to
his prayer request! He immediately bowed down and
worshipped God.

The servant was offered shelter at Abraham's relatives house
and offered a meal. However, the servant refused to eat until
he explained his mission. After hearing his story, Rebekah's
father and brother agreed to the marriage. The servant told
of Abraham's wealth and their eyes gleamed with
excitement at the parade of camels bearing beautiful gifts of
clothing and fine jewelry. There was joy in the house as they
celebrated the upcoming marriage. Rebekah's future looked
bright as the wife of Abraham's only son and heir to his

fortune.

> *And they blessed Rebekah, and said unto her, thou*
> *art our sister, be thou the mother of thousands of*
> *millions, and let thy seed possess the gate of those*
> *which hate them. (Genesis 24:60)*

With tears in her eyes and excitement in her heart, Rebekah left her family's home to start her new life. Her nurse, Deborah, was sent along to help Rebekah.

As they traveled, Rebekah's mind was preoccupied with thoughts of Isaac. What did he look like? Was he kind? Did he have a good sense of humor? Images of family and children danced in her head. She looked forward to her new life and future marriage.

It was early evening when Rebekah arrived in her new hometown. As a handsome young man approached the caravan, she dismounted her camel and covered her face. I imagine this act was similar to a virgin bride walking down the aisle to be joined with her groom.

Isaac took Rebekah into his mother's tent and she became his wife. He fell in love with her and she loved him back. Isaac was no longer lonely. Giving love and being loved helped to heal Isaac's heart after his mother's death.

> *And Isaac was forty years old when he took Rebekah to*
> *wife, the daughter of Bethuel the Syrian of Padanaram,*
> *the sister to Laban the Syrian. (Genesis 25:20)*

At this point in their story, Isaac and Rebekah have been married for 20 years.   Although they never used birth control, they had no children and being childless was a stigma in those days. Rebekah remembered her family's blessing: "be thou the mother of thousands of millions." Well, that blessing had not come true. At this point, she would be content being the mother of one.

> *And Isaac intreated the LORD for his wife, because she was barren: and the LORD was intreated of him, and Rebekah his wife conceived. (Genesis 25:21)*

Rebekah's cycle was late, and she wondered…is it possible? She would not allow her mind to go there and she blocked it out saying, "I'll just wait and see, because this has happened before."

Another week passed, and then three weeks passed, and two months passed, and she decided to believe that what she wanted so much was really happening to her. Oh happy, happy day when her pregnancy was confirmed by nurse Deborah!

Isaac and Rebekah were overjoyed. Isaac thanked God for answering his prayer and placed his hand on Rebekah's stomach with a smile. Rebekah proudly rubbed her belly bump and smiled too. She was happy, downright elated…and then it happened.

Rumble, rumble, bump, bump, kick, kick. Rebekah wailed in

pain, "Ooooowwww! Oh, my goodness, what is going on? Oh God, no, please no. Don't let me lose this baby. God please, help me."

Panic-stricken Rebekah quickly called her nurse, and she came running. After the examination and the news of no threatened miscarriage, Rebekah's mind was at ease. The baby was extremely active, and she was instructed to take it easy.

From that day forward, Rebekah had a rough pregnancy. She was in constant discomfort. She was tired, worn out and miserable. The nurse didn't know what was going on. Every single day it felt like a war going on inside Rebekah's womb. There was so much movement, punching, kicking - and boy did it hurt!

Rebekah must have wondered, "why me, Lord, why me?" She was so uncomfortable that she cried out "Lord why is this happening to me?"

God answered her cry. She was a little surprised by the answer, but it made perfect sense and explained everything.

The Lord said "You are pregnant with two nations in your womb. One will be stronger than the other and the older will serve the younger."

Two nations, two types of people. Two nationalities in one womb. Two different looking sons, two different thinking sons, two different destinies – one stronger than the other, older will serve younger.

Rebekah now understood the war in her womb. It seemed logical that her boys would struggle and wrestle in her womb. Although she understood the sibling rivalry, she wished the fighting would stop!

Time passed, and Rebekah could hardly wait to deliver the two fighting nations in her womb. It had been a long, hard and exhausting pregnancy. The day of delivery arrived accompanied by intense labor pains. Then with one final push, Rebekah delivered her first son. He was a handsome little red boy with thick hair all over his body. To nurse Deborah's surprise there was a hand on the heel of this little boy. It was as if the other baby was trying to pull him back in or trying to propel himself out. He held on with a tight grip and would not let his brother's heel go until he too entered the earth's atmosphere and breathed his first breath. He had smooth skin and was strong.

Isaac and Rebekah were very proud parents. Esau was the name of their hairy first-born son and the heel holding second-born son they named Jacob.

The twin boys were as different as night and day. The Bible does not tell about their youth, the verse after their birth simply says, "the boys grew." Esau became a skillful hunter and Jacob liked to stay home and cook.

Jacob was a momma's boy and a great cook. His older brother Esau was his dads' favorite and he was a hunter. One day, Esau was on his way home from a hunting trip. He was famished and could smell the savory aroma of stew from miles away. That smell led him straight to the pot where Jacob was stirring his stew.

> *"And Esau said to Jacob, feed me, I pray thee, with that same red pottage; for I am faint: therefore, was his name called Edom."*
>
> *And Jacob said, sell me this day thy birthright.*
>
> *And Esau said, Behold, I am at the point to die: and what profit shall this birthright do to me?*
>
> *And Jacob said, swear to me this day; and he sware unto him: and he sold his birthright unto Jacob. (Genesis 25:30-33)*

Jacob let Esau know from the start that his stew wasn't free – and it wasn't cheap. There was a price tag attached to Jacob's stew and if Esau was not willing to pay, then he would have to eat something else. The stew was very pricey; in fact, it was the most expensive stew Esau would ever eat because it cost his birthright. The birthright was a future blessing of the first-born son; it was his inheritance.

Esau was very weak and hungry. He felt like he was going to die if he didn't eat right away. He told Jacob that the future birthright was of no value to him if he was dead from starvation. Jacob made Esau swear that the birthright belonged to him and in a state of hunger, he sold his birthright to Jacob. After agreeing to the terms and conditions, Esau had a very satisfying portion of Jacob's delicious stew.

In Genesis twenty-seven, many years had passed, Isaac grew older and became blind. With his health failing, and unable to see, he decided it was time to give Esau the birthright blessing.

Isaac and Esau had a great relationship. In honor of this auspicious occasion, Isaac made a request of his first-born son. He wanted Esau to go hunting and make some of his delicious fresh venison stew to accompany the special birthright blessing. As they made plans to celebrate the day, Rebekah stood outside the tent and quietly listened to their private conversation. When Esau left to go hunting, Rebekah got busy.

That birthright belonged to Jacob, and Rebekah was going to make sure that her favorite son received it. Rebekah and Jacob devised an elaborate scheme to deceive Isaac.

Jacob was instructed to go outside, kill two young goats and keep the skin. Rebekah made some of the good old savory stew that Isaac loved. She then had Jacob dress in Esau's shirt. To complete the scam, she carefully weaved the hairy goatskin to Jacob's smooth skin. To a blind man, Jacob would feel and smell like Esau.

Dressed to deceive and with the good smelling stew in his hands, Jacob went to Isaac's tent. From the very first greeting, Isaac was suspicious of the son serving him stew. His hearing was still intact and though the son in the tent said he was Esau, the voice sounded smooth like Jacob's. Isaac was blind, but he was not a fool.

Filled with suspicion, Isaac instructed his son to come closer, so he could touch him and verify he was in the presence of Esau. Isaac touched Jacob's goatskin covered hands and relaxed a little bit. Whew, Jacob passed that test! The delicious stew was served and next on the schedule was the birthright blessing.

Isaac enjoyed the stew, but he was still skeptical of the son serving him stew. He had one final request before the blessing. He asked his favorite son for a kiss. As Jacob kissed his father, Isaac deeply inhaled and then relaxed as he smelled the familiar scent of Esau. Isaac concluded that his mind was playing tricks on him, so he let down his guard and gave Jacob every blessing he had to give under the sun. Jacob was relieved and quickly left the tent.

As soon as Jacob left, Esau arrived carrying a piping hot dish of stew. He was in a good mood and expected to receive his father's blessing. What he heard was unbelievable to his ears - all his inheritance had been given to his lying twin brother Jacob. This big, burly, rugged hunter was so devastated by the news that he literally broke down and cried.

Esau was furious, and his anger reached the boiling point. He was full of rage and wanted Jacob dead! The one thing that kept Esau from committing murder that day was his respect for Isaac. With simmering anger and vengeance in his heart, he thought of various ways to remove his brother from the earth. Esau believed that his father would die soon and after mourning the death of his father, he planned to bury Jacob too.

Rebekah heard about Esau's plot to kill his brother and interceded on Jacob's behalf. She convinced Isaac that Jacob needed to go back to her hometown, to her family and find a good wife because the local girls were not an option. This was a good idea to Isaac because it worked so well for them. The matter was settled, and Rebekah was relieved. Jacob escaped Esau's death trap and went to live in his mother's hometown with her relatives.

After leaving home, Jacob spent 20 years working for his uncle Laban. During this time, he acquired wives, sons and a daughter. In Genesis 31:3, the Lord told Jacob to return home. As he neared his hometown, he sent a note to his brother Esau announcing his return. In response to this greeting, Esau and 400 of his men set out to meet Jacob who was terrified and prepared for the worst. To Jacob's surprise, Esau was glad to see him, he was no longer angry, and the sting of Jacob's deception was in the past.

Although not recorded in the Bible, I believe Jacob went home as God instructed. I wonder if Rebekah was still alive when he returned home? I don't know the answer to that question, but if she was alive, can you imagine the joy in her heart as she laid eyes on Jacob and his caravan of wives, children, servants, and livestock? Envision Rebekah squinting her eyes trying to identify the images off in the distance. Could it be? Is it possible? Jacob! If it happened, undoubtedly that was one of the best days of Rebekah's life.

The Bible does not record the death of Rebekah. In Genesis 35:8 nurse Deborah died, but by this time she was traveling with Jacob and his family. How did Rebekah's personal nurse end up traveling with Jacob's family? Did she go with Jacob after Rebekah's death? Is it possible that nurse Deborah accompanied Jacob as he escaped Esau's death grip?

The answers to these questions would give us more insight into Rebekah's death. However, the Bible only records that Rebekah was buried in a place of honor with her husband Isaac in the family cave along with Abraham and Sarah. (Genesis 49:31)

Notes

_____

_____

_____

_____

_____

_____

_____

_____

_____

_____

_____

_____

_____

_____

_____

_____

_____

Notes

_____

_____

_____

_____

_____

_____

_____

_____

_____

_____

_____

_____

_____

_____

_____

Chapter 3

Tricked into Destiny

Abraham begat Isaac; and Isaac begat Jacob; and Jacob begat Judas and his brethren; (Matthew 1:2)

Jacob escaped Esau's death grip and traveled to his mother's home town. As he approached his destination, he saw shepherds in a field near a well waiting to water their sheep. Jacob struck up a conversation with them, inquiring about his relatives and to his surprise they knew his family. What are the odds? On top of that, his cousin Rachel was headed that way to water her sheep.

Jacob sprang into action. He removed a huge rock that was covering the mouth of the well and watered Rachel's sheep. Filled with gratitude that he found his mother's family, he kissed Rachel and cried aloud.

When uncle Laban found out that his nephew was in town, he hurried out to greet him. There he embraced him, kissed him and welcomed him into their home. Jacob shared his life's story and Laban said, "you really are my own flesh and blood." (Genesis 29:14 NLT)

Jacob was handy and did a lot of work for his uncle Laban. After about a month's time, his uncle offered to pay him and ask Jacob how much did he want to be paid. I'm sure Jacob had been thinking about this, and he responded, "I'll work for you for seven years if you'll give me Rachel, your younger daughter, as my wife." (Genesis 29:18b NLT) Laban had two daughters, the beautiful Rachel and her older sister Leah. Jacob was in love with Rachel.

It was a deal! Laban agreed to give Rachel to Jacob in exchange for working seven years. His uncle said he would rather give her to Jacob than any other man. Rachel was everything Jacob desired in a wife.

The news was out - Rachel was getting married. Rachel was happy, buzzing around like a little honey bee. She hummed and danced and smiled. She talked to Leah about Jacob nonstop. Oh, how she loved that man and Jacob loved her too. Leah was happy for her baby sister, yet she fantasized about her own wedding someday.

Jacob completed the seven years of laborious work for his beloved Rachel. The greatly anticipated day had finally arrived. While the bride and groom were preparing for the blessed nuptials, this is what I imagine happened:

Scene 1: (Rachel's bedroom)

Rachel: (wakes up, smiling, happy) …What a wonderful day…I am so happy. (opens closet and screams) …Where is my dress?

Maid: (hurriedly enters the room) …Your father has it and he want to see you.

Rachel: (relieved)…Oh, daddy! (exits)

Scene 2: (Leah's bedroom)

Laban: Leah, I have something for you

Leah: Oh, father, a gift for me... (takes gift) ...it's not my birthday... (looking at Laban) ...I love surprises!

Laban: This one is rightfully yours.

Leah: (opens the gift, excited) ...oh its embroidered... (removes from box) ...it's mother's wedding dress... (smiling, but confused)

Laban: It should fit you perfectly.

Leah: Yeah, but.

Laban: All of your attendants will be here soon to help you put it on.

Leah: No daddy, I'm wearing...

Laban: (interrupts)...This dress.

Leah: But I'm not getting married.

Laban: (firmly) Yes, you are.

Leah: (concerned)... I know you're a little older now daddy, but you're really starting to scare me.

Laban: (holds her by her shoulders...kisses forehead) You will be a good wife.

Leah: (pushes back) ...Hold it dad...stop it! (firm) It's

Rachel's wedding day…not mine.

Laban: No…(firm)…tonight Leah, you will marry Jacob!

Leah: No dad, I'm not marrying Rachel's man.

Laban: I'm telling you this one-time Leah. Arrangements have been made between me and Jacob…and besides…I'm not going to let a long-distance relative come here and upset the way we do things…you know we don't do stuff like that around here.

Leah: Daddy, what are you talking about?

Laban: Don't play with me, Leah. You know we don't marry off the youngest girl before the oldest one is married…it's just not happening.

Leah: But dad, what about Rachel?

Laban: Rachel is not your concern.

Leah: But she is my little sister and she loves Jacob…(sobbing)

Laban: Snap out of it Leah…I'm doing this for you. You've never had a boyfriend and your prospects are none. Now, pull yourself together and get ready for your wedding! (exits)

What an imaginary scene! The morning after the wedding, Jacob woke up in marital bliss holding Rachel in his arms. He kissed her forehead as the morning light dawned and fell upon the face of the not so lovely cousin Leah. Why was she in his bed? Where was the love of his life, Rachel? He quickly arose from the marriage bed. Stumbling and tripping and holding his tunic, Jacob ran out of the tent. He never noticed that he left Leah embarrassed and in tears. Leah cried alone and felt sorry for herself. How she longed to talk to Rachel, but that was impossible now. From that day forward, Leah and Rachel were at odds. Their loving sisterhood was now reduced to sibling rivalry.

When Jacob confronted his uncle Laban, he was educated on the laws of the land. It was customary for the oldest daughter to be married first and then the younger daughter, not the other way around. He was given another opportunity to marry his beloved Rachel. If he worked another seven years for her hand, she would be his second wife. Feeling tricked, helpless and out of options, Jacob consented to the new contract.

Jacob was advised to finish his honeymoon week with Leah and after that, he could marry Rachel too. Laban made sure that Jacob took care of Leah and performed his husbandly duties with her. Within the span of a week, Jacob had two sister wives, Leah and Rachel.

Leah was jealous of Jacob and Rachel's relationship because she was unloved. She cringed every time she saw them laughing, holding hands, smiling and kissing. She felt like a third wheel, she was just in the way, but on the other hand, it was her right to be Jacob's wife.

Leah was not the chosen wife; she was more like a booby prize. How do you imagine Leah felt? Genesis 29:32-35 tells us exactly how she felt. It says Leah was afflicted. She was in mental distress, unhappy, sad, and lonely. She was aggrieved, hurt, angry, and upset. Should I go on? She was wounded, injured, and tormented. She felt unloved, rejected, and disrespected. Having those feelings can make you hard, cold, and bitter.

God saw that Leah was hated and He decided to open her womb. When Jacob performed his husbandly duty, Leah got pregnant and had a son. She named the baby boy Reuben which means "see, a son." It was like she was saying "see Jacob, I gave you a son. Don't you love me now?" She thought Jacob would love her for giving him a son. Leah waited for Jacob's love and acceptance, but their relationship remained the same.

Leah was very fertile, and she gave Jacob another son. She named this son Simeon which means "God heard." What did God hear? God heard her pain, he heard that she was hated, he heard her distress, he heard that she was sad, lonely, wounded, injured, and tormented. He heard!

Being a fertile, baby-making machine Leah got pregnant again and had another son. She was tickled pink. She was convinced that the third son was the charm. This time for sure Jacob would be joined to her and named her son Levi, which means "attached." Needless to say, Jacob was still devoted to his beloved Rachel.

Still enjoying her marital bed with Jacob, Leah got pregnant again and had a son. This time she decided to praise God and named him Judah. She turned her attention from her husband and herself to focus on God. Every time she called her son Judah, she was saying "Praise God!"

Being a mother to four handsome boys was Leah's pride and joy. After birthing Judah, she stopped getting pregnant. Leah was jealous of Rachel because Jacob truly loved her, and Rachel was jealous of Leah because she was so fertile and kept giving her husband babies. Rachel was unable to have children and there was a constant rivalry between the sister wives.

Rachel decided to give Jacob to her maid Bilhah as a wife. Just like Sarah, she wanted Bilhah to be a surrogate mother for her and she would raise the child as her own. Jacob obliged the request, married Bilhah and impregnated her. She gave him a son whom Rachel named Dan which means "vindicated." She said she was vindicated because God heard her request. Bilhah got pregnant again and had a second son whom Rachel named Naphtali, which means "my struggle." Rachel said she struggled hard with her sister and now she is winning!

When Leah realized she was no longer getting pregnant after several encounters with Jacob, she decided to give her maid Zilpah to Jacob to be a surrogate mother for her. Zilpah birthed two sons, the first Leah named Gad which means "good fortune"; and the second son she named Asher which means "happy."

Years passed, and Leah's oldest son Reuben gathered mandrakes in a field and brought them home to his mother. Rachel was desperate and wanted to be pregnant by any means necessary. She humbled herself and begged Leah for some of Reuben's mandrakes because these fruits were rumored to have fertility-enhancing properties.

Leah fired back. She basically said, "you've taken my man, now you want to take my son's mandrakes?" Rachel threw in her trump card and said, "you can sleep with Jacob tonight in exchange for your son's mandrakes!" That was music to Leah's ears and the exchange was made.

Leah prepared herself and her bedroom to receive her husband that night. She dressed up and met Jacob as he came home from work that day. She said, "you're coming home with me tonight." As Jacob fulfilled his husbandly duty, Leah got pregnant again! She had a fifth son and named him Issachar which sounds like a Hebrew term meaning "reward." Leah thought this son was God's reward for giving her maid to Jacob.

Leah had a sixth son for Jacob and named him Zebulun. This time she thought her husband would give her honor and respect. Zebulun probably means "honor." After a period of time, Leah had a daughter named Dinah and stopped having children.

In my mind's eye, Leah was a great mom and poured all of

her love into her children like many single mothers do today. Although she was a married woman, I believe most of Jacob's time was spent with Rachel and not Leah or her children. With the constant bickering and rivalry among his wives, I seriously doubt if Rachel permitted Jacob to spend a lot of time at Leah's place. Most men value peace, and Jacob probably kept his primary home peaceful by spending much of his time with Rachel, which is where he wanted to be.

Leah named each son according to what she wanted or hoped to get from her husband. With Reuben, she wanted to be loved. With Simeon, she found solace in the fact that God heard her misery. With Levi she wanted Jacob to be attached to her and devote some time to her. With Judah, Leah decided to Praise God.

Leah learned many life lessons through her relationship with her husband. It was very clear to her that having babies by a man does not make him love you or be devoted to his children. She and her children were well taken care of financially but lacked the close relationship with Jacob they desired.

Leah wanted a real head over heels type of love that she never received from her husband. She was rejected by Jacob but chosen by God.

Jacob tricked Esau and stole his birthright. Laban tricked Jacob to marry Leah instead of Rachel. Jacob and Leah were tricked into destiny. By God's design, Jacob was ordained to be the third name in the patriarchal dynasty of Abraham,

Isaac, and Jacob - the founding fathers of the Jewish nation. It was also God's design that Leah be honored as his first wife. Jacob didn't choose Leah, God did.

The not so beautiful, overlooked and unwanted Leah has a remarkable place in Biblical history. Have you ever heard of the Lion of the Tribe of Judah? Well, Leah is Judah's mother. Although her name does not appear in Matthew chapter one, Leah was destined to be a part of the royal bloodline of Jesus Christ through their fourth son Judah, "Praise God!"

Leah's death is not mentioned in the Bible. Genesis 49:31 speaks of Leah's body being laid to rest in the place of honor due to the first wife. When Jacob is near death, he instructs his son to bury him in the cave with Abraham and Sarah, Isaac and Rebekah, and his first wife Leah.

Notes

_____

_____

_____

_____

_____

_____

_____

_____

_____

_____

_____

_____

_____

_____

_____

_____

_____

Notes

_____

_____

_____

_____

_____

_____

_____

_____

_____

_____

_____

_____

_____

_____

_____

Chapter 4

Playing Tricks

And Judas begat Phares and Zara of Thamar; and Phares begat Esrom; and Esrom begat Aram; (Matthew 1:3)

NOTE: Names in bold print signify the featured story characters in the King James Version of the Bible. Modern translations of names are used for Judah and Tamar.

Tamar is the first named woman in the ancestry of Jesus. We have talked about Sarah, Rebekah and Leah being part of this story, but their names do not appear in the Matthew one text at all. Tamar's name does.

We are introduced to Tamar in Genesis thirty-eight, as a young bride. She was married to Judah's first-born son Er. Their marriage didn't last very long because Er died. Tamar was devastated by his death. She was a sad young widow with no children to love or to prolong Er's legacy. However, Tamar still had a chance to become a mother and contribute to future generations because of her brother-in-law, Onan.

Then Judah said to Er's brother Onan, "Go and marry Tamar, as our law requires of the brother of a man who has died. You must produce an heir for your brother." (Genesis 38:8 NLT)

Onan married Tamar. He knew the law required him to have children with her in honor of his dead brother. Onan had a problem with that law and decided to partially obey it. He kept the part of the law he liked (having sex with Tamar) but refused to comply with the part he didn't like (raising an heir for his brother). While he enjoyed having sex on a regular basis with Tamar, every time he was about to reach climax he pulled out. Over a period of time, Onan also died. Tamar was a childless widow, again.

This devastated young woman had lost two husbands. She mourned for each of them and felt sorry for herself. Her dream of being a wife and a mother was deferred, yet she was confident that one day she would have an heir to carry on the family legacy. Unfortunately, now was not the time. She had to be patient and wait, hoping that motherhood would one day be a reality.

> *Then Judah said to Tamar, his daughter-in-law, "Go back to your parents' home and remain a widow until my son Shelah is old enough to marry you." (Genesis 38:11a NLT)*

Judah was saddened by the death of his two oldest sons. He missed them terribly. He and his family mourned their deaths. The only son he had left was his youngest boy, Shelah, whom he held close to his heart.

Judah sent Tamar home to her family and told her to remain a widow until Shelah was old enough to marry her. Tamar did as she was told and every day she put on drab clothing to signify her widowhood.

Several years passed as Tamar waited for her youngest brother-in-law to become old enough to marry. She knew his birthdate and she counted down the years. Boy how she looked forward to being married again.

While Tamar waited for Shelah to mature a tragic event occurred. Her mother-in-law passed away and Tamar mourned her death. She wished she could have spent more time with her and wished she could have given her grandchildren.

Finally, it was Shelah's birthday. Her youngest brother-in-law was old enough for marriage! Tamar was full of hope and started to get excited about being a wife and hopefully a mother. Every day she looked for a message from Judah announcing the date of their marriage. Time passed, the message never arrived, and Tamar was mad.

Tamar's simmering anger started to boil upon realizing she had been tricked. It was clear that Judah had no intentions of letting her marry Shelah. Living the rest of her life as a childless widow was not an option. Tamar was young and full of life. She absolutely refused to be denied another opportunity to become a mother. She came up with a plan and took matters into her own hands.

Since her mother-in-law was dead, Tamar knew Judah would be horny and looking for some action. Her plan was simple, all she had to do was make it available. When she heard that her father-in-law was coming to town she put her scheme into action. Draping a veil across her face, and dressed like a prostitute she stood on the corner and waited to seduce Judah.

> *"So, he stopped and propositioned her. "Let me have sex with you," he said, not realizing that she was his own daughter-in-law."*
>
> *"How much will you pay to have sex with me?" Tamar asked. "I'll send you a young goat from my flock," Judah promised.*
>
> *"But what will you give me to guarantee that you will send the goat?" she asked. "What kind of guarantee do you want?" he replied.*
>
> *She answered, "Leave me your identification seal and its cord and the walking stick you are carrying." So, Judah gave them to her. Then he had intercourse with her, and she became pregnant. (Genesis 38:16-18 NLT)*

When the deed was done, Judah and Tamar parted ways. Tamar knew playing tricks as a prostitute could have deadly consequences – especially if it worked and she got pregnant. Oh, how she hoped and prayed that she was pregnant!

Tamar was quick-witted and smart. She skillfully negotiated a contract whereby she would retain Judah's personal identification as a guarantee that he would later send payment in the form of a goat. However, Tamar didn't want a goat! The payment she wanted was already in her hands.

Judah had every intention of paying his debt. He sent the goat by a friend to the same corner he found the prostitute standing on, but she wasn't there. He asked the local men where to find her and they claimed there was never a regular prostitute on that corner. The friend returned with the goat and Judah didn't want to look like a fool trying to find her again, so he decided to let the prostitute keep what she had.

Months passed, and Judah heard that Tamar was pregnant. He was irate! She "played the harlot" and disgraced his family's name! This was an outrage, she had simply gone too far. With righteous indignation, Judah gave the order to have his prostituting daughter-in-law burned!

> *But as they were taking her out to kill her, she sent this message to her father-in-law: "The man who owns these things made me pregnant. Look closely. Whose seal and cord and walking stick are these? (Genesis 38:25 NLT)*

Judah's mouth dropped wide open as he shook his head in disbelief. He was so embarrassed because he immediately recognized his own things. Filled with shame, he had his daughter-in-law released from death's grip. His seal, his cord, and his cane saved Tamar's life. Judah now understood the motives for her deception and admitted that she had acted more righteous than he had.

Finally, Tamar was going to be a mother and gained the respect of her father-in-law. Judah moved Tamar back into his house, but he never had sex with her again.

Tamar became the first named woman in the ancestry of Jesus when she had twin boys, Perez and Zerah, by her father-in-law Judah.

Notes

_____

_____

_____

_____

_____

_____

_____

_____

_____

_____

_____

_____

_____

_____

_____

_____

_____

_____

Notes

Chapter 5

Clever Girl

*And Salmon begat Booz of Rachab; and Booz begat
Obed of Ruth; and Obed begat Jesse; (Matthew 1:5)*

NOTE: The name in bold print signifies the featured story
character in the King James Version of the Bible (KJV). A
modern translation of Bible is used for the name Rahab.

The next named woman in the ancestry of Jesus is Rahab.
She enters the scriptures in Joshua chapter two, as the
Israelites are on their way to the promised land.

Rahab lived in Jericho which was a city surrounded by a tall,
thick wall. It stood between the Israelites and the promised
land. This city had to be conquered and its wall had to fall!
With plans to attack Jericho, Joshua sent two men to spy out
the land. Just inside the city, the spies entered a house built
on the wall. It was a house of ill repute that belonged to a
harlot named Rahab.

The people of Jericho heard the Israelites were coming their
way and rumors were circulating around the city about the
mighty power of their God. There were fantastic stories of
God fighting for the Israelites and drying up the Red Sea. It
was reported that God destroyed kings and nations. The
people of Jericho were petrified, and Rahab instinctively
knew that Jericho was doomed!

When the Israelite spies entered Rahab's house, she

welcomed them with open arms. Bombarded with thoughts racing through her mind, she decided to barter with the spies. Rahab was well versed in the politics of Jericho. She anticipated the king's men would come looking for the spies, so she decided to hide them on her rooftop. As expected, the king's men came to Rahab's house. When questioned about the spies, she lied and put her life on the line. She claimed she didn't know who the men were or where they had gone, but one thing she knew for sure was that they left (^the) city before the gate closed. Armed with misinformation, the king's men immediately left Rahab's house in hot pursuit of the spies.

Rahab waited a while after their departure and then she went to the rooftop to have a conversation with the spies. She said to them:

> *"For the LORD your God is the supreme God of the heavens above and the earth below."*

> *"Now swear to me by the LORD that you will be kind to me and my family since I have helped you. Give me some guarantee that when Jericho is conquered, you will let me live, along with my father and mother, my brothers and sisters, and all their families." (Joshua 2:11c-13 NLT)*

In addition to being brave enough to put her life on the line, Rahab was a clever girl. She did the spies a favor by saving their lives and now she wanted a guarantee they would do the same for her. The two men agreed if the following conditions were met:

- Keep a scarlet rope hanging in the window.

- Have her people inside her house when Israel attacked the city.

- Keep their agreement a secret.

That was great news for Rahab and she gladly consented to the conditions. Whew, what a relief! Her quick wit and fast action paid off. Now she could rest assured that she and her family would be safe when her hometown was destroyed.

Rahab hung a red scarlet rope from a window and allowed the spies to escape. Per the spies' instructions, this rope was never to be removed from the window. It was their sign of agreement. The house on the wall with a red rope hanging from the window was a safe place – everything inside that house will be saved when Jericho is destroyed.

In Joshua chapter six, the Israelite army prepared to invade Jericho. The people of Jericho were horrified. Death and destruction were on the other side of the tall thick wall that surrounded the city. With each trumpet blast, the thick wall seemed to reverberate, and the people's confidence was shaken.

Rahab quickly gathered her family inside the house and closed the door. She could hear the sounds of marching soldiers and trumpet blasts – and then there was silence.

This went on for six days and the people of Jericho were afraid and confused. As the soldiers marched around the city, they saw the red rope hanging from a window and remembered their agreement with Rahab.

On day seven, Jericho was awakened by the sound of marching footsteps. Anxiety levels were heightened as the Israelite Army changed their pattern and continuously marched around the city. This was the day they feared the most – doomsday.

With a long blast of trumpets and a mighty loud shout, the thick walls of Jericho suddenly fell. There was nowhere to run and nowhere to hide. The Israelites attacked the city and destroyed everything in sight, men, women, boys, girls, infants, sheep, goats, donkeys, cats, and dogs. The only people left alive in Jericho were those inside the house with the red scarlet rope hanging from the window – Rahab's house. Rahab's clan grabbed everything they could carry and joined the Israelites. Once her family was safely outside the city, Joshua gave the order to burn Jericho down and the entire thick-walled city was reduced to rubble. Rahab and her family continued with the Israelites to the promised land. With her whore house destroyed and a fresh new start, Rahab retired from prostitution. She caught the eye of an Israelite man named Salmon whom she eventually married, and they raised a family. Rahab is the mother of the famous biblical character that, so many women are looking for today. She is the mother of Boaz and the second named woman in Matthew chapter one in the ancestry of Jesus.

Notes

Notes

Chapter 6

Dedicated Soul

DEDICATED SOUL Chapter 6

And Salmon begat Booz of Rachab; And Booz begat
Obed of Ruth; and Obed begat Jesse; (Matthew 1:5)

NOTE: Names in bold print signify the featured story characters in the King James Version of the Bible (KJV). A modern translation of Bible is used for Boaz.

The next named woman in the ancestry of Jesus is Ruth. Unlike Tamar and Rahab, Ruth wasn't a prostitute and she wasn't shrewd or even cunning.   She was the type of woman I would expect to be a part of Jesus' ancestry – except for a few things – she wasn't Jewish, and she was previously married.

Ruth had high moral standards. She was loyal, she loved hard and deep. She was committed and had a dedicated soul.   We are introduced to Ruth when Elimelech and his Jewish family moves into her neighborhood.

> *"Now it came to pass in the days when the judges*
> *ruled, that there was a famine in the land. And a*
> *certain man of Bethlehem Judah went to sojourn in*
> *the country of Moab, he, and his wife, and his two*
> *sons."*
>
> *And the name of the man was Elimelech, and the*
> *name of his wife Naomi, and the name of his two*
> *sons Mahlon and Chilion, Ephrathites of*

Bethlehemjudah. And they came into the country of
Moab, and continued there. (Ruth 1:1-2)

Due to the severe famine in Bethlehem, Judah, a Jewish man named Elimelech moved his family to Moab. Unfortunately, while there, he died leaving behind his wife Naomi and their two sons Chilion and Mahlon.

As life continued, their two sons married Moabite women. Chilion married Orpah and Mahlon married Ruth. Ten years passed, and tragedy struck this family again. Chilion and Mahlon both died leaving three widowed women to fend for themselves. Times were hard for these women. Naomi was now the head of the house and had to look out for her daughters-in-law. When she heard there was food in Bethlehem, she decided it was time to go back home. The three women packed up what they could carry and set out on their journey.

On the way to Bethlehem, Naomi stopped in the road to bless her daughters-in-law Orpah and Ruth. She wished them well and hoped they would find security in the home of another husband. With that, she released her daughters-in-law to return home to their families.

Over the years these women had grown to love each other deeply, they had become a real family. Together they had lived, loved and laughed. They talked, prayed and cried together. There were times when they held hands and shared empathizing hugs of comfort as each of them experienced widowhood.

These women had been a strong support for each other. They understood what it was like to experience lonely wedding anniversaries, broken-hearted birthdays and uncelebrated holidays. Their hearts were knit together in love, life, and death. Ruth and Orpah were more than daughters-in-law to Naomi, they were her daughters.

Naomi suffered more than the other women because she lost all the men in her family – her husband and two sons. The thought of saying goodbye to these women who held such a special place in her heart was very painful, but Naomi wanted to do what was best for her daughters. The women embraced, and buckets of tears raced down their cheeks as they cleared their throats to speak.

Orpah and Ruth vowed to go home with Naomi, but their futures looked very bleak as she had nothing left to offer them. She had no prospects for a husband and even if she married today, would they live as widows waiting for her newborn sons to mature? No, the sacrifice was too much to ask of any attractive young woman.

Right there at the fork in the road, each woman decided the course of her future. After long hugs and sobs, Orpah agreed with Naomi's logic and kissed her goodbye. She sadly walked away, constantly looking back, waving and crying. Sometimes she walked backward gazing at her family as she took the road back home to Moab.

As they watched Orpah disappear into the distance, Naomi noticed Ruth was still clinging to her arm. Ruth was strongly encouraged to follow Orpah's example and go back to her family's house and her gods.

> But Ruth replied, *"Don't ask me to leave you and turn back. Wherever you go, I will go; wherever you live, I will live. Your people will be my people, and your God will be my God. Wherever you die, I will die, and there I will be buried. May the LORD punish me severely if I allow anything but death to separate us!" When Naomi saw that Ruth was determined to go with her, she said nothing more. (Ruth 1:16-18 NLT)*

When Ruth and Naomi arrived in Bethlehem, they had very little. Ruth was a survivor and was not content hanging around the house doing nothing. She went out and found work in a barley field where she picked up a few handfuls of grain other workers left behind. Ruth worked hard and seldom took a break. She was determined to take care of herself and Naomi.

It was Ruth's first day on the job and she had worked for hours when Boaz, the landowner, arrived. As he looked over his crop, he noticed an unfamiliar woman working in his field. When he asked his workers about her, he was told that she was the foreigner who came to Bethlehem with Naomi. "Ah-ha," Boaz could now put a face to the stories he heard about Naomi's daughter-in-law.

The news circulated around town that Naomi had returned to Bethlehem. People said that she looked frazzled, worn and frail. The old image of the happy-go-lucky Naomi with a loving husband and two handsome sons was replaced by this barely recognizable person. When they saw her, the people asked, "is that Naomi?" The woman who left town with a caravan had now returned a poor, childless widow.

Naomi endured the stares and whispers of the town's people who wondered "who is that woman with Naomi?" They learned that her name was Ruth. She was Mahlon's widow.

Naomi was bitter because she had nothing left to offer anyone. Despite this fact, Ruth refused to allow Naomi to walk out of her life. Ruth was good to Naomi and good for Naomi. They shared precious memories and moments of silence. They were not alone, they had each other, and they were very grateful for that.

Boaz heard of Ruth's love and dedication to Naomi. He heard that she left her family and her gods to live with strangers here in Bethlehem. He also heard that she was a good support for Naomi, who happened to be his relative.

> "Boaz went over and said to Ruth, "Listen, my daughter. Stay right here with us when you gather grain; don't go to any other fields. Stay right behind the young women working in my field. See which part of the field they are harvesting, and then follow them. I have warned the young men not to treat you roughly. And when you are thirsty, help yourself to the water they have drawn from the well." Ruth fell at his feet and thanked him warmly. "What have I

done to deserve such kindness?" she asked. "I am only a foreigner."

"Yes, I know," Boaz replied. "But I also know about everything you have done for your mother-in-law since the death of your husband. I have heard how you left your father and mother and your own land to live here among complete strangers.

"May the LORD, the God of Israel, under whose wings you have come to take refuge, reward you fully for what you have done."

"I hope I continue to please you, sir," she replied. "You have comforted me by speaking so kindly to me, even though I am not one of your workers." (Ruth 2:8-13 NLT)

From that time forward, Boaz looked out for Ruth. At mealtime, he invited her to lunch. Ruth ate roasted grain until she was fully satisfied, and she even had enough left over to take home to Naomi.

Boaz ordered his male workers not to bother Ruth. He told them to notice where she was working and allow her the freedom to pick grain wherever she wanted to pick it. They were also instructed to drop handfuls of grain on purpose in her path, so she could pick them up.

Ruth worked all day and when she beat out the grain that evening she was elated. She hurried home to Naomi and showed her the day's bounty. They were excited! Ruth picked an entire 5-gallon basketful of grain in one single day!

Naomi enjoyed roasted grain and listened closely to her daughter-in-law recount the events of the day. Ruth was absolutely overwhelmed by the kindness and generosity of the landowner named Boaz. Naomi's appetite was satisfied. She smiled and told Ruth that Boaz was a close relative. Ruth told Naomi that Boaz invited her to work only in his field until the harvest was complete.

> *"Good!" Naomi exclaimed. "Do as he says, my daughter. Stay with his young women right through the whole harvest. You might be harassed in other fields, but you'll be safe with him."*

> *So, Ruth worked alongside the women in Boaz's fields and gathered grain with them until the end of the barley harvest. Then she continued working with them through the wheat harvest in early summer. And all the while she lived with her mother-in-law. (Ruth 2:22-23 NLT)*

Throughout the spring and summer, Ruth worked in Boaz's fields. Day after day, she continued to bring home good quantities of grain. While Ruth worked, Naomi thought about the future.

Dramatization

Ruth returns home after working all day in the field.

Naomi: I've been thinking.

Ruth: What have you been thinking about mom?

Naomi: I think it's time to find a good home for you, so you can have a happy life.

Ruth: Life's not so bad, we have a place to stay and food eat.

Naomi: It's more to life than that…and girl you work too hard.

Ruth: I don't mind working.

Naomi: I know you don't mind working, but I want to make things so much better for you.

Ruth: How are you going to do that?

Naomi: You've been working in Boaz's field, right?

Ruth: That's right.

Naomi: You know that Boaz is our close relative.

Ruth: Yes, you mentioned that before.

Naomi: Well, I think it's time to make our move.

Ruth: (Puzzled) What move?

Naomi: Tonight, Boaz will be working at the threshing floor.

Ruth: Oh, he's working tonight?

Naomi: Un-huh. Here's what I want you to do. Take a bath…

Ruth: Take a bath?

Naomi: Un-huh. Put on some perfume.

Ruth: Put on perfume?

Naomi: Un-huh. Put on this dress.

Ruth: This dress?

Naomi: Un-huh.

Ruth: Oh, this is a beautiful dress.

Naomi: After you get all dressed up, go down to the threshing floor.

Ruth: Momma, you want me to go down to the threshing floor in this dress?

Naomi: Un-huh.

Ruth: What!?

Naomi: Listen now.

Ruth: I'm listening.

Naomi: When you get to the threshing floor be very quiet.

Ruth: Okay.

Naomi: Get close enough so you can see Boaz as he works

Ruth: Huh?

Naomi: Listen now. Be sure to watch him and see where he goes to sleep.

Ruth: You want me to stalk Boaz?

Naomi: Well.... un-huh! Wait till he's sleeping, then go and lie at his feet.

Ruth: (shocked) Mama Naomi, you want me to lie at his feet?

Naomi: Un-huh. That's letting him know you're available for marriage.

Ruth: (hopeful) Oooohhhhh, I like that idea.

Naomi: Then just wait…he'll tell you what to do.

Ruth: Alright, I'll do everything you said.

Ruth followed Naomi's instructions to the letter. Dressed up and smelling good, she arrived at the threshing floor. She watched Boaz and waited for him to fall asleep. She took a deep breath and put the plan into action. She uncovered Boaz's feet to lie down. As he turned over in the middle of the night he was startled to find a woman lying at his feet. Ruth was nervous, but she had enough courage to complete her task and asked Boaz to spread the corner of his garment over her. She was asking him to provide for her and to redeem her. Simply put, Ruth asked Boaz to marry her.

Boaz knew just what to say to calm Ruth's nerves. Essentially, he said "Ruth, don't be afraid. I'll do everything you ask, but you have a close relative who has first options of redeeming you. I will follow protocol and see if he is willing to marry you. Don't worry Ruth, if he does not redeem you - I will!"

Ruth breathed a sigh of relief and had a glimmer of hope in her eyes. Boaz never sent Ruth away from his presence empty-handed. As she prepared to leave, he gave her six big scoops of barley to share with her wise mother-in-law Naomi.

Early the next morning Boaz was about the business of redeeming Ruth. He found that close relative, explained the situation to him...and...the relative politely declined to marry Ruth. With that, Boaz knew exactly what to do. He immediately found Ruth and made her his wife.

The matchmaking mother-in-law was ecstatic. Although Naomi didn't have another son to marry Ruth, her close relative Boaz was willing to redeem her. By redeeming Ruth, Boaz agreed to buy the land belonging to Naomi's family and he also agreed to raise children in the name of Ruth's deceased husband. Ruth now has a chance to become a mother and Naomi a grandmother!

Ruth became pregnant and had a son they named Obed. It's interesting to note that Ruth was married many years to

Mahlon, but never conceived a child. It was God's plan that Ruth married Boaz. The town's people now called Naomi blessed and said Ruth was better to her than seven sons. Naomi was content and satisfied as she held little Obed at her breasts.

Ruth was destined to be in the ancestry of God's only Begotten Son. She is the great-grandmother of King David. You may read her entire story in the book of the Bible titled after her "Ruth." She is one of only two women to have this honor. In Matthew chapter one, Ruth is the third named woman in the ancestry of Jesus Christ.

Notes

Notes

Chapter 7

The Cover Up

And Jesse begat David the king; and David the king begat Solomon of her that had been the wife of Urias; (Matthew 1:6)

NOTE: Names in bold print signify the featured story characters in the King James Version of the Bible (KJV). Modern translations of Bible used for the wife of Uriah.

The next woman Matthew chapter one mentions in the ancestry of Jesus is the wife of Uriah. Uriah was a soldier in the Israelite Army. In fact, he was in the Special Forces and one of King David's "37 elite soldiers." He was married to a beautiful woman named Bathsheba.

We are introduced to Bathsheba in 2nd Samuel chapter eleven when she was taking a bath. She had just completed the purification rites after having her menstrual cycle. As you know, bathing is a private moment and Bathsheba had no idea she was being watched by the king!

A short time after she finished bathing, there was a knock at her door. To her surprise, there stood a royal messenger who gave her a summons to appear before the king! Not next week or even tomorrow, but right now! Imagine the thoughts running through Bathsheba's mind... What did I do? Why does the king want to see me? Uriah! Is Uriah okay?"

Bathsheba nervously entered the palace and bowed before the king. King David extended his hand, and some of Bathsheba's anxieties disappeared. She had never been so close to the king before. She noticed that he was very handsome with beautiful eyes, but she felt a bit uncomfortable because of the king's lustful stares.

It became blatantly clear to Bathsheba that she was not summoned to the king's palace because something was wrong...no...she was summoned to the king's palace for the king's pleasure...and who could say "no" to the king? As Bathsheba surrendered to the king's sexual advances she could smell the fresh scent of his hair and the sweet-smelling musk from the sweat of his body.

After her encounter with the king, Bathsheba was taken home. The ride seemed unusually long, and she thought of her husband Uriah. If he had been home instead of fighting in the king's war, this never would have happened! Oh, how she missed Uriah.

Bathsheba had a difficult time comprehending the fact that she just slept with the King of Israel. Tears ran down her face as she washed his scent from her skin. Her emotions were all over the place. She was ashamed of the evening's events, yet she was flattered the king found her irresistible.

Time passes and memories of her encounter with the king are constantly on her mind. What happens if Uriah finds out? Bathsheba worries but tries to push that thought out of her head. She anxiously awaits her menstrual cycle, but there is no sign of it, not even a friendly "cramp." Months pass, and Bathsheba confirmed that she was pregnant. She nervously sent a message to the king. This was an awkward situation for her because she hadn't been with her husband in a long time. How in the world could she explain this to Uriah?

Bathsheba was pregnant by King David, the most powerful man in the land...but she was worried about her relationship with her husband, a soldier in the king's army. She knew the king had to take care of this situation, after all, his reputation was on the line too.

King David summoned Uriah from the battlefield on the pretense of needing a status update on the war. Uriah gathered his thoughts and gave the king a detailed account of the war. After Uriah gave the report, the king dismissed him to go home and get some rest. In King David's mind, this was the solution to his problem. Certainly, Uriah was anxious to get home to show his young, beautiful, voluptuous wife how much he missed her. David thought to himself, "after tonight's encounter with Bathsheba, Uriah will certainly think that he was the father of her child."

The king slept very well that night, but the next morning he was alarmed when he heard that Uriah didn't go home. Uriah was a dedicated soldier and couldn't bear the thought of making love to his wife while his fellow soldiers were at war. He absolutely refused to enjoy the comforts of home, so he slept at the palace gate with the king's servant.

David's next move was to invite Uriah to dinner. He got him drunk and tried to send him home again to his wife, but that didn't work either.

When King David realized Uriah had no intentions of going home to Bathsheba, he decided to send him back to war. In the few short days David spent with this soldier, he learned that he was a dedicated soldier, loyal to the king and the Israelite Army. David saw no other option but to use his loyalty as a snare.

The king wrote a letter and told Uriah to deliver it to the captain of his army. Uriah gladly took the letter and immediately headed back to war to fight in King David's Army. David relied on the fact that Uriah was a man of strong character and he would not look at the letter, besides that it bore the king's seal. Little did the messenger know that the letter he carried and delivered with his own hands contained the strategic details to end his life!

Bathsheba anxiously awaited to hear from the king. One day there was a knock at the door, and there stood the king's messenger. This time the message stated, "we regret to inform you that your husband Uriah was killed in battle." Bathsheba broke down and cried, she mourned for Uriah. She felt guilty and relieved at the same time, but she would never have wished this for Uriah.

After the time for mourning Uriah was over, Bathsheba moved into the palace to become King David's wife...and their secret was safe. Months later Bathsheba gave birth to a precious baby boy. Like any mom, Bathsheba was amazed at the miracle she held in her arms. The love she had for her baby boy was like none she had ever experienced in her life! He became the love of her life! After all, she didn't really love David, and Uriah, her husband was dead.

One day the baby got sick…and the doctors didn't know how to cure him. Bathsheba's heart ached as she held him close and constantly cried and prayed for him. King David was upset. He laid on the floor praying and crying and refusing to eat.

The baby died seven days after the illness began, and Bathsheba was broken. She felt the baby's death was punishment for their sin. She blamed herself for this and she blamed David. She was sad and mourned deeply for the loss of her first-born son.

David and Bathsheba cried together, and they comforted each other. As they lay together, she became pregnant and birthed Solomon. She had a total of four sons for King David, with Solomon being the most famous.

In Matthew chapter one, King Solomon is the offspring that carries on the lineage of Jesus Christ. However, recorded in Luke 3:31, David's son Nathan becomes a part of Jesus' ancestry. In 1st Chronicles 3:5 Bathsheba is bestowed double honor as she is the mother of both these men.

It is of special note that some biblical scholars believe the genealogical account of Jesus' ancestry in the book of Luke is the Virgin Mary's lineage. This may be one of those unanswered questions that we will understand when Jesus returns.

Although unnamed in Matthew chapter one, Bathsheba is referred to as "wife of Uriah" in the ancestry of Jesus Christ.

Notes

Notes

Chapter 8

The Pregnant Virgin

THE PREGNANT VIRGIN

And Jacob begat Joseph the husband of Mary, of whom was born Jesus, who is called Christ. (Matthew 1:16)

This is the story of a young teenage girl named Mary. She was a good girl and loved by all. She was engaged, but still a virgin.

Mary was home alone probably doing whatever a normal Jewish teenage girl would be doing on any given day. This day was different because suddenly out of thin air an angel appeared. Mary was frightened. One minute she was home alone and the next second standing in front of her was an angelic being from heaven.

The angel Gabriel who stands in the presence of God Himself appeared to a mere mortal human being. He enthusiastically greets this girl with words of high praise "hail, the Lord is with you, highly favored, blessed among women."

Quite naturally Mary was uneasy with the angel's sudden appearance and, she wondered "what kind of hello is this?" She questioned his statements "The Lord is with me?" and "I'm blessed and highly favored?"

There were many thoughts racing through Mary's head. To ease the anxiety in her heart, the angel said "Don't be afraid.

You have favor with God."

The tension in Mary's neck started to ease and suddenly she felt at peace. The angel went on to complete his assignment by telling Mary that she was going to have a son named Jesus and He was going be great! God was going to give him King David's throne! He would rule forever, and His kingdom will never end!

Mary was again intrigued by the angel's words and the possibility of having such a powerful son, but she was confused. She asked the angel, "how can this happen? I've never been with a man."

The angel Gabriel assured Mary that no man will touch her, and she will remain a virgin until after the birth of her son. He told her that God's Holy Spirit will overshadow her, and she will conceive a holy child. This baby will be the Son of God.

The angel didn't stop there. He gave Mary more proof of God's ability to do the impossible. Gabriel told Mary that her cousin Elisabeth was pregnant. I imagine Mary gasped with surprise. She was aware of the fact that Elisabeth and John really wanted children, but were never able to have them and now they were old, really old. She knew the ache in her barren cousin's heart and now with this news, she was happy for Elisabeth.

After the enthusiastic angelic greeting, the promises of a bright future, and the miraculous conception of cousin

Elisabeth, Mary said "yes." With the offer accepted and the assignment complete, the angel disappeared into thin air as quickly as he appeared.

Imagine being a young, single virgin having a conversation with an angel who said God wants you to birth His child. Who can you share that information with?

God knew that Mary would need a place of solace. He understood that Mary's mind would explode with all kinds of "what if" questions after her angelic visitation. What if Joseph calls off the wedding? What if I'm pregnant with no husband? What if I'm kicked out of the house? What if I'm ashamed and embarrassed? What if they think I'm crazy? What if they call me a liar? What if...

After days of pondering the angel's words, Mary felt so much pressure that she wanted to get away – away from Joseph, away from her family and away from her friends. Where could she go and who would believe her?

Mary recalled the angel's words and knew exactly where to go. Cousin Elisabeth's house! Mary wanted to celebrate her pregnancy and...cousin Elisabeth would understand her dilemma.

Elisabeth was six months pregnant at the time of Mary's visit. As Mary entered the house and said hello, the baby in Elisabeth's womb jumped and she was filled with the Holy Spirit. As the Spirit of God moved upon Elisabeth, she proclaimed, "Blessed art thou among women and blessed is the fruit of thy womb."

The presence of the Holy Spirit was in the house! Mary and Elisabeth had a grand old time praising God for who He is and the miraculous way He honored them. They were elated and thankful for God's blessings in their lives. They hugged, they shouted, they sang, they cried, they praised God with all their might. While they worshipped, John the Baptist joined in and rejoiced in his mother's womb.

This visit was a dose of good medicine for these two pregnant women of destiny. It confirmed the words spoken by the angel. Mary found a place of peace, comradery, and comfort at Elisabeth's house. The "what ifs" in her head were silenced. Elizabeth found comfort in the presence of another pregnant woman. She shared her fears and hopes as well as her stories of morning sickness, tender breasts and movement in her womb.

Neither woman was trying to conceive a child when God decided to change the course of their lives. Elisabeth was an old, married, barren woman who ceased having menstrual cycles and thought she would never conceive. Mary, on the other hand, was an engaged teenage virgin who dreamed of being a mother someday in the future. God implemented the unexpected, but necessary changes in these women's lives were essential to accomplish His plan and His purpose. God chooses whomever He wants to choose, and His timing serves His purpose.

Mary stayed with Elisabeth about three months. On her

return home, Mary was prayed up and strong. She had proof that the angel's words were true: three missed menstrual cycles, morning sickness, enlarging breasts, strange cravings, and snug fitting clothes.

God was aware of Mary's character before He chose her for this most sacred assignment. She was honest, trustworthy, reliable and had strong faith. God was confident that Mary would not try to deceive Joseph by making him think that he was the father of her child. With all her heart Mary loved God, but this pregnancy placed her in a very precarious situation. She was now the blushing bride-to-be with a bump.

Mary loved Joseph and looked forward to being his wife. Now that her pregnancy was confirmed, she needed to have a serious talk with her fiancé. Mary understood there was a great risk of rejection, yet she felt compelled to tell Joseph of her angelic visitation.

As Joseph listened to the entire story from beginning to end, one word "pregnant" reverberated in his mind. To say the least, Joseph was shocked because Mary was a sweet, honest – virgin? He did not believe the angelic visitation and the immaculate conception story. Joseph truly loved Mary and thought he was going to spend the rest of his life with her, but he didn't bargain for this.

Did Mary really expect him to go through with the wedding and watch her belly swell with another man's baby!? What was he supposed to do?

Joseph was hurt, but he decided to deal with this situation in a manner that was best for the both of them. He didn't want to publicly embarrass Mary and he didn't want to raise another man's child, so he decided to quietly call off the wedding. The matter was settled in Joseph's mind and he went to sleep.

While sleeping, Joseph had a dream. He envisioned an angel who gave him clear, direct, and precise instructions. He said, "son of David, don't be afraid." With his heart and mind open, Joseph listened intently as the angel spoke of miraculous things to come. Joseph had heard these things before because the angel was confirming everything Mary said. He was instructed to go through with the planned wedding ceremony, and when the baby was born to name him "Jesus." The angel told Joseph that this marriage was ordained by God. He said it was intertwined with the fulfillment of a great prophecy, "Behold, a virgin shall be with child and shall bring forth a son, and they shall call his name Emmanuel, which means, God with us."

Joseph woke up from his sleep and realized that indeed God was with him. The dream was so real! He experienced an angelic visitation and now believed in immaculate conception. He was ready to get married and was no longer concerned about raising another man's child. Joseph embraced the fact that his marriage to Mary was ordained and he was honored that God had chosen him to be called the earthly father of Jesus.

When it was time for Jesus to be born, Mary and Joseph were traveling. They stopped at an inn, but all the rooms were taken so they took shelter in a barn. When Jesus was born, Mary wrapped him tightly and laid him in a feeding trough for animals. She held him, loved him, cherished him and raised him. In Matthew chapter one, Mary is the last, but certainly not least, named woman in the ancestry of Jesus Christ, our Lord, and Savior.

Notes

_____

_____

_____

_____

_____

_____

_____

_____

_____

_____

_____

_____

_____

_____

_____

_____

Notes

_____

_____

_____

_____

_____

_____

_____

_____

_____

_____

_____

_____

_____

_____

_____

_____

Notes

_____

_____

_____

_____

_____

_____

_____

_____

_____

_____

_____

_____

_____

_____

_____

_____

Chapter 9

The Hall of Faith

But without faith it is impossible to please him: for
he that cometh to God must believe that he is, and
that he is a rewarder of them that diligently seek
him. (Hebrews 11:6)

The 11th chapter of Hebrews is sometimes referred to as
"The Hall of Faith."   It tells the stories of patriarchs and
matriarchs who saw miracles in their lives because they
combined their faith with action.

I've come to realize that God continues to speak in a still,
small voice, that is so discreet sometimes I overlook it. Little
by little, I'm learning to be obedient to the quiet whisper I
hear in my spirit. When God speaks, we are to recognize His
voice and obey it by faith. This book started with a blog post
and has been written by faith. Its impact on society is yet to
be seen.

By faith old man Abraham believed he would father a child
and he did at the age of one hundred years old. By faith,
Sarah received strength to conceive, carry and deliver
Abraham's son at the age of ninety.

By faith, Isaac prayed for his infertile wife Rebekah to
conceive a child after twenty years of marriage. By faith,
Rebekah birthed twin boys who were two nations
developing in her womb. As per the prophecy, Jacob, the
younger one, was stronger than his older brother Esau. By

faith, Jacob took his birthright and his name completes the patriarchal lineage of "Abraham, Isaac, and Jacob." By faith, Leah married Jacob and gave him six boys and a girl. Their son Judah became the fourth patriarch in the ancestry of Jesus in Matthew chapter one.

By faith, Judah took Tamar home and never "touched" her again. By faith, Tamar birthed twin boys by her father-in-law Judah and became the first named woman in the ancestry of Jesus in Matthew chapter one. Their son Perez is the fifth patriarch in the lineage of Jesus in this same chapter.

By faith, Rahab hid the Israelite spies and saved her family's lives. By faith, Salmon married a retired prostitute who was destined to become the second named woman in Matthew chapter one in the ancestry of Jesus.

By faith, Ruth left her family and her gods to follow her mother-in-law Naomi to an unknown land. By faith, Boaz married Ruth and they became the father of Obed and the great-grandparents of King David.

By faith, King David relied on the mercy of God to forgive his sin. By faith, Bathsheba married King David and birthed King Solomon and Nathan. She is mentioned as "the wife of Uriah" in the ancestry of Jesus.

By faith Mary, mother of Jesus agreed to God's plan for her life and said, "be it unto me according to thy word." By faith, Joseph married a virgin who was pregnant with God's Son.

The rewards of faith may not be fully seen or appreciated in one's lifetime. Like Abraham, Isaac, Jacob and the rest of the ancestors of Jesus, the benefits of our faith continue through generations following us. Our faith in God has great rewards! The benefits of our faith will shower blessings on our children and their children and their children's children throughout eternity.

Conclusion

Conclusion

As I contemplated the bloodline of Jesus, I thought His ancestors would have been saints. In my imagination, God would only allow those with royal, holy blood to have the privilege of being in Jesus' earthly lineage.

Here is a list of my three prerequisites to even be considered a possible candidate for the lineage of God's Holy and Righteous Son. Only those applicants passing this criterion would be permitted to move on to the next phase of conditions:

- Jewish people with high moral values who were as close to sinless as possible.

- Faithful men with only one wife – no divorcees or widows.

- Faithful women with one husband – no divorcees or widows.

- Both male and female candidates would practice celibacy until their wedding night.

Out of all the ancestors of Jesus, I would say Ruth and Mary were among the most upstanding and honorable female members in His family tree. As you can see from my prerequisites above, I would have disqualified Ruth because she was not a Jew and she was previously married.

Trying to determine who would be a great candidate for the

bloodline of Jesus is mentally exhausting and I'm glad God didn't consider my opinion when He made that decision.

The patriarchs and matriarchs of the Bible had no idea the impact their lives would have on the world. The thought never crossed their minds that they would be the "stars" of the Bible. They lived their lives as they saw fit. They made good judgment calls, sometimes; and trusted God, sometimes. They were just like we are today.

The Bible records the actual life stories of the men and women in the ancestry of Jesus. These stories highlighted the celebratory events in their lives as well as their sneaky, deceptive and sinful deeds.

I imagine Jacob, David and Tamar would hang their heads in shame due to some of their actions recorded in the Bible:

- Jacob lied to his father and stole his brother's birthright.

- David had an affair with a married woman and ordered her husband's death to conceal it.

- Tamar purposefully dressed like a hooker and slept with her father-in-law.

God did not hide the sordid details of these people's lives. In fact, He placed them on the front page of the New Testament in the Bible. This novel is based on some of the characters in Matthew chapter one whose lives have been the topic of many sermons and books. As we read their stories, we form conclusions and make judgment calls. I must warn you to be careful judging these characters as the stories of our lives are still being written today.

What if your story is being recorded and God uses it in His next book? Would you be a main character like Abraham, David or Ruth? Maybe your character would be a supporting cast member like Sarah, Rebekah, and Leah. Would your story encapsulate one single life event like Rahab's or would it detail years of living like Jacob's?

If God has another book and it's anything like His first, it will expose events we would rather leave concealed. His book would include modern stories of drug users, dope dealers, and women who aborted babies; as well as the age-old stories of rapists, adulterers, prostitutes, thieves, and murderers.

When our stories are told, we don't want to be remembered as a "character." We want to be remembered as real living and breathing human beings with strong feelings and convictions. Life is not a fairytale, and neither are the stories of Jesus' ancestors. These people lived. They loved, they laughed, and they cried.

Jesus' earthly ancestors had issues. Some were liars, cheaters, prostitutes, and murderers. Some were selfish and only concerned with self-preservation. After all, they were just like you and me - human!

I believe God revealed their dirty little secrets to show His love for us and His patience with us. Their stories tell us that we are not the first to mess up and we won't be the last. Despite their sins and shortcomings, these people were still a part of God's plan. It's worth noting that God did not change His mind about their destiny when they messed up. He used flawed, sinful, conniving men and women to be the ancestors of His Only Begotten Son. No matter where we are or what we have done, God still has a good plan for our lives.

Through these stories, I believe God is saying that Jesus came down through the lineage of sinners' blood to save sinners' souls. Jesus came to save His mother, His earthly father, His grandmother, and grandfather, and all those ancestors tracing back to the pure bloodline of Adam. Jesus' sacrifice also provides salvation for the future unborn generations scheduled to be birthed into the earth's atmosphere at their appointed time. Yes, Jesus came down through royally sin-filled blood to save the world from sin.

ALWAYS REMEMBER

God LOVES YOU...no matter what you've done!

If you are feeling guilty about events in your life, talk to God. Ask Him to forgive you and forgive yourself.

Life is a gift and how we choose to live it is our gift to God. So, live life to the fullest and remember - God is watching!

Notes

_____

_____

_____

_____

_____

_____

_____

_____

_____

_____

_____

_____

_____

_____

_____

Notes

_____

_____

_____

_____

_____

_____

_____

_____

_____

_____

_____

_____

_____

_____

_____

Notes

_____

_____

_____

_____

_____

_____

_____

_____

_____

_____

_____

_____

_____

_____

_____

_____

Notes

_____

_____

_____

_____

_____

_____

_____

_____

_____

_____

_____

_____

_____

Contact Us

For speaking engagements, bulk book purchases and any additional comments or concerns, please feel free to connect with me at:

info@alicenewsome.com

or connect with me on my social media page

https://www.facebook.com/alice.newsome.505

http://bit.ly/2yqMPlX

For all your video production needs, please visit our social media site at:

https://www.facebook.com/eagleeyevideomaker

At Eagle Eye Video,

we record conferences, and events for all occasions.

www.ingramcontent.com/pod-product-compliance
Lightning Source LLC
Chambersburg PA
CBHW072200090426
42740CB00012B/2328